**DISCARD**

# Deshaun WATSON

Property of CLPL

Tammy Gagne

A ROBBIE READER

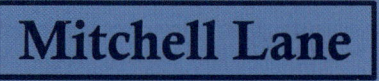

**PUBLISHERS**

2001 SW 31st Avenue
Hallandale, FL 33009

www.mitchelllane.com

Copyright © 2020 by Mitchell Lane Publishers. All rights reserved. No part of this book may be reproduced without written permission from the publisher. Printed and bound in the United States of America.

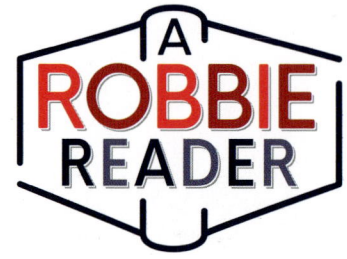

First Edition, 2020.
Author: Tammy Gagne
Designer: Ed Morgan
Editor: Lisa Petrillo

Series: Robbie Reader
Title: Deshaun Watson / by Tammy Gagne

Hallandale, FL : Mitchell Lane Publishers, [2020]

Library bound ISBN: 9781680205169
eBook ISBN: 9781680205176

PHOTO CREDITS: Design Elements, freepik.com, Getty Images

# Contents

**one**
The **NEXT GENERATION** — 4

**two**
A **HOME** of **THEIR OWN** — 8

**three**
A **STRONG ARM** and **SPIRIT** — 12

**four**
An **EARLY COMMITMENT** — 16

**five**
**GOING PRO** — 20

| | |
|---|---|
| Timeline | 28 |
| Find Out More | 29 |
| Works Consulted | 29 |
| About the Author | 32 |

# CHAPTER ONE

# The NEXT Generation

"What time do you need to be at football practice Saturday?" Grant's mom asked. She was scrolling through her calendar computer application as she joined him at the kitchen table. "I can drop you and Michah off if his mom can pick you up."

"We don't have practice Saturday morning," Grant said, gulping down the hot cocoa she had made the two of them. He hugged his mug with both hands. The October air had already turned cold, and his fingers were still freezing from taking out the garbage after dinner.

"No practice?" She looked up from reading on her smartphone. She figured she had heard him wrong. "Don't you have a playoff game on Sunday?"

"Yup," he replied. "The coach bumped our practice to the afternoon. We are spending the morning volunteering for Habitat for Humanity."

"You are going to help build houses?"

"Well, little ones. We are building birdhouses for new homeowners. The coach talked to us about the importance of giving back to our community. The birdhouses will be ready the same day the families get their house keys."

"What a great idea," his mother said. "I've read some interesting things about that organization."

"Like what?"

# CHAPTER ONE

"Well, did *you* know that one of your favorite NFL (National Football League) players is a spokesperson?" She was referring to Deshaun Watson, quarterback for the Houston Texans.

"I did," Grant replied. "Did you know that Watson actually grew up in a Habitat for Humanity home? He also received the first Next Generation award from the organization in 2015. It is for kids of Habitat homes who go on to achieve great things."

"I didn't know that," his mother admitted. "It sounds like your coach chose a great way for your team to give back."

"Actually, I suggested the idea. The coach asked everyone to come up with ways we could give back. I learned about Habitat for Humanity in an article I read about Watson. So I went to the organization's website and found directions for building the birdhouses there."

"You know," Grant's mother said, "I think you just might go on to do great things yourself, kiddo."

Watson's goal is always to get the ball in the end zone.

## CHAPTER TWO

# A HOME of their Own

**Derrick DeShaun Watson** was born on September 14, 1995, in Gainesville, Georgia. His mother Deann Watson was a single parent. Derrick's father was not in the picture. His older brother Detrick was five years old when Derrick joined the family. The boys' twin siblings, Tinisha and Tyreke, hadn't been born yet.

The only home Deann could afford was government housing for low-income families. The apartment complex wasn't the most kid-friendly setting. Many of the Watsons' neighbors were gang members or drug dealers. Deann didn't even feel safe letting her children trick-or-treat in their own neighborhood on Halloween. Instead, she took them to a church event that offered candy for kids in costume.

When the family returned home, Deann carefully inspected all the treats before letting her kids eat them. In the process she came across a flyer for Habitat for Humanity. It explained how people who were willing to work hard could end up with their own house from the organization. No one was willing to work harder for it than she was. She performed nearly 300 hours of **community service**. She even helped build houses for three other families.

## CHAPTER TWO

Derrick was 11 years old when his family received their house from Habitat for Humantiy. By then he was in middle school and going by his middle name, Deshaun. Former Atlanta Falcons **running back** Warrick Dunn volunteered his time to come to the celebration. An avid volunteer for the organization, made famous

An important hero to young Deshaun was Atlanta football star Warrick Dunn, left, shown here playing for the Falcons in 2006.

Deshaun Watson has always felt right at home on a football field.

Deshaun continued to excel at football when he entered high school. Skipping the junior varsity team altogether, he began playing on his school's varsity team his very first year. Gainesville High School Coach Bruce Miller told a reporter for the Bleacher Report, "Going into his freshman year, we went to camp and some of the things he did against other teams, it was just unbelievable for a freshman."

## CHAPTER THREE

While Deshaun was in high school, his mother got sick. Deann Watson went to the doctor, sure she had strep throat. But it turned out that she had a more serious illness—tongue cancer. She did not want her kids to see her while she endured **chemotherapy** and **radiation** at Emory University Hospital in Atlanta. The doctors eventually had to remove part of her tongue, and it took a while for her to learn to speak again.

Watson celebrates with his aunt Suzette (*left*) and mother, Deann.

# A Strong Arm and Spirit

Deshaun's aunt and uncle stepped up to take care of the kids while Deann was away. They all missed their mother terribly. Deshaun only saw her two of three times during his entire sophomore year. After the long battle, Denna won the fight. In a 2016 interview with a reporter for the Watch Stadium sports network, Deshaun shared an update on his mother's condition. "She's cancer free and living life to the fullest."

Like his mother, Deshaun never gave up. He kept his nose in the books and worked hard on the football field. As a junior, he helped the Gainesville High Red Elephants win the state championship. When he graduated in 2013, he ranked as the number one high school quarterback in the United States. He finished his high school career with 13,077 yards, 155 passing touchdowns, and 59 rushing touchdowns. These impressive stats earned him the title of *USA Today* High School Sports All-American.

## CHAPTER FOUR

# An EARLY *Commitment*

**When the time came** to make college plans, Deshaun Watson had many options. **Recruiters** from several colleges wanted him to play for them. Scouts began watching him as early as his freshman year at Gainesville High. Even national sportswriters knew who Watson was. Watson showed tremendous instincts as a player, that was the first thing reporter Rusty Mansell of 247Sports website noticed about the future football star. "The ball just jumps out of his hand when you see him throw," Mansell told a reporter for the Bleacher Report. "I remember thinking the sky is the limit for this guy."

Watson visited colleges in Alabama, Florida, Tennessee, and of course, Georgia. But he ended up choosing Clemson University in South Carolina, a college with a strong football legacy. He was still a sophomore when he made the decision to become a Clemson Tiger. Not many tenth-graders receive such offers, or commit to one so early. But Clemson was willing to build its football program around Watson. He later told a reporter for ESPN that this was the deciding factor for him.

Watson was making a name for himself in football as early as high school and college.

## CHAPTER **FOUR**

Watson didn't waste any time getting things done on the Clemson field. He played in the season opener, which the Tigers played against the Georgia Bulldogs. In that game he threw a 30-yard touchdown. It was one of two passes he completed in the game, for a total of 59 yards. Three weeks later, Watson broke a team record. He threw six touchdown passes in a game against the University of South Carolina. If Clemson had any doubts about offering Watson a spot while he was so young, they could now be put to rest.

*The strong work ethic that Deshaun's mother had instilled in him was paying off at Clemson University.*

# An Early Commitment

## CHAPTER FOUR

The following year, Watson led Clemson to win the Atlantic Coast Conference (ACC) title. By now he had made a habit of breaking records. This time he scored the most touchdowns in an ACC game—five total for the game. His hard work earned him a third-place finish in the voting for the Heisman Trophy, one of the most famous national awards given annually to an athlete considered the most outstanding in college football. The next year he finished second for the honor after leading the Tigers to a national championship against the University of Alabama.

The football field wasn't the only place Watson was giving things his all. Just a few months into his junior year of college, Watson earned the final credits toward his degree in communications studies. He became the first person in his family to earn a college degree, and he had accomplished the impressive task in just three years. With college now behind him, he decided it was time to pursue his next goal, entering the 2017 NFL Draft.

Commissioner of the ACC, John Swofford and Watson celebrating after winning the ACC Championship with his Clemson Tigers.

# An Early Commitment

## CHAPTER FIVE

# GOING *Pro*

**The 2017 NFL Draft** took place in April in Philadelphia. Deshaun Watson headed to the event with great enthusiasm. The Houston Texans made a deal with the Cleveland Browns to get the twelfth pick of the first round. Houston officials used their pick to select Watson. In a fun **coincidence**, Watson's mentor and friend, Warrick Dunn, had been drafted twelfth overall back in 1997.

Watson throws a pass defended by Myles Jack of the Jacksonville Jaguars in September 2017.

Much like his high school **debut**, Watson made it onto the field to play in his very first NFL game. The team was struggling in its season opener against Jacksonville. The coach decided to replace the starting **quarterback**, Tom Savage, with Watson at halftime. Although the Texans lost that game, Watson played well. He helped his new teammates with their next game. And in his next five games, he threw a total of 18 touchdown passes.

## CHAPTER **FIVE**

Watson seemed to be on track for another incredible season. But an injury in November cut his rookie season short. During practice he tore his knee joint, the anterior cruciate ligament (ACL). He needed surgery followed by intense **rehabilitation**. He would not set foot on the field again until the following season.

People immediately started talking about what Watson would do next. Fellow NFL player Richard Sherman told a reporter for TheMMQB.com, "By next year he's going to be a top-five quarterback in this league, and that includes the two big dogs (Tom Brady and Aaron Rodgers). He makes you dig to the deepest part of your competitive juices to beat him."

*After tearing his ACL, Watson worked hard to get back on the field as soon as possible.*

# CHAPTER FIVE

As much as fans look to Watson's future, he makes sure to remember the past as well. He sports tattoos on his forearms that include a deck of playing cards, a pair of dice, and his state championship ring with the number 815 inside it. The images remind him that he must play the cards he is dealt, and that doing so always comes with a bit of luck. The number was part of his first address in government housing: 815 Harrison Square. As Watson told a reporter for ESPN, "It reminds me of where everything started."

# Timeline

**1995** — Derrick Deshaun Watson is born September 14.

**2006** — His family receives a house they helped build from Habitat for Humanity.

**2010** — He earns the quarterback spot for Gainesville High as a freshman.

**2012** — Deshaun leads his high school team to the state championships.

**2013** — He commits to attend Clemson University to play college ball.

**2014** — He graduates from Gainesville High.

Becomes starting quarterback for Clemson.

**2015** — Watson and his Clemson teammates win the ACC title.

**2016** — He leads Clemson to its first national title.

Watson graduates early with a bachelor's degree in communications studies.

**2017** — He enters the NFL Draft. The Houston Texans select him as the No. 12 pick.

# Find Out More

"Deshaun Watson." EPSN
http://www.espn.com/nfl/player/_/id/3122840/deshaun-watson

Houston Texans website
https://www.houstontexans.com/

NFL website
https://www.nfl.com/

Morey, Allan. *Superstars of the Houston Texans*. Mankato, MN: Amicus Ink, 2019.

Koehn, Rebecca. *Behind the Scenes of Pro Football*. North Mankato, MN: Capstone Press, 2019.

**Works Consulted**

"Deshaun Watson Opens Up On Mom's Cancer Battle: 'She's Living Life To The Fullest.'" *Watch Stadium*, August 30, 2016.
https://watchstadium.com/news/deshaun-watson-mom-cancer-08-30-2016/

"Hands-on building projects." Habitat for Humanity.
https://www.habitat.org/volunteer/near-you/youth-programs/resources/hands-on-projects

"Watson details Warrick Dunn's impact on his life." *EPSN*.
http://www.espn.com/video/clip?id=18371548

Adams, Jonathan. "Deshaun Watson's Family: 5 Facts You Need to Know." May 18, 2017.
https://heavy.com/sports/2017/04/deshaun-watson-who-mom-cancer-family-photos-dad-mother-warrick-dunn-father-brothers-sister/

**Works Consulted** *continued*

Bonesteel, Matt. "Deshaun Watson went No. 12 in the NFL draft. Here's why that's pretty amazing." *Washington Post*, April 28, 2017.
https://www.washingtonpost.com/news/early-lead/wp/2017/04/28/deshaun-watson-went-no-12-in-the-nfl-draft-heres-why-thats-pretty-amazing/?utm_term=.ba9b70cfda8f

Hale, David M. "How a house became a home for Deshaun Watson." *ESPN*, October 3, 2015.
http://www.espn.com/college-football/story/_/id/13780893/deshaun-watson-giving-back-organization-community-gave-chance-following-dreams

Kirpalani, Sanjay. "The College Recruitment of Deshaun Watson." *Bleacher Report*, December 23, 2016.
https://bleacherreport.com/articles/2679324-the-college-recruitment-of-deshaun-watson

McQuade, Alec; Reed, Kristen; and Pearl, Matthew. "Timeline of a champion: Deshaun Watson." *11 Alive*, January 10, 2017.
https://www.11alive.com/article/sports/timeline-of-a-champion-deshaun-watson/384829878

Roberts, John. "An extraordinary start, interrupted: Deshaun Watson by the numbers." *ESPN*, November 2, 2017.
http://www.espn.com/nfl/story/_/id/21253097/nfl-extraordinary-start-interrupted-deshaun-watson-numbers

Tsuji, Alysha. "Deshaun Watson gave his mom a brand new Jaguar days after being drafted by Texans." *USA Today*, April 29, 2017.
https://ftw.usatoday.com/2017/04/deshaun-watson-new-car-mom-texans-nfl-draft-clemson-quarterback-family-jaguar

# Glossary

**chemotherapy**
A treatment for cancer made of chemicals that kill the cancer cells

**coincidence**
Two or more events that seem related but happen by chance

**community service**
Time spent performing work for charity

**debut**
A person's first public appearance in a particular setting

**quarterback**
A football player who directs the offense of the team

**radiation**
A cancer treatment which uses high-energy particles or waves

**recruiter**
A person who looks for talented athletes

**rehabilitation**
The process of recovering use of the human body following an injury or illness

# Index

| | |
|---|---|
| 2017 NFL Draft | 20, 22 |
| Clemson University | 17–20 |
| Dunn, Warrick | 10–11, 22 |
| Gainsville | 8, 11, 13 |
| Gainesville Red Elephants | 15–16 |
| Habitat for Humanity | 5–6, 9–11 |
| Houston Texans | 6, 22–23 |
| Sherman, Richard | 24 |
| Watson, Deann | 8–9, 14–15 |
| Watson, Deshaun | |
|   charity work | 6 |
|   education | 15, 20 |
|   injury | 24 |
|   records | 18, 20 |
|   tattoos | 26 |
| Watson, Detrick | 8 |
| Watson, Tinisha | 8 |
| Watson, Tyreke | 8 |

# About the Author

**Tammy Gagne** has written more than 200 books for both adults and children. As a lifelong New Englander, her loyalty lies with the Patriots. But her work has led her to count several other boys of fall among her favorites over the years. Her most recent titles also include *Todd Gurley* and *Jason Tatum*.